Saving My Son

119 DAYS OF SMALL MIRACLES
BEHIND THE NICU DOORS

IMA D. CARNELUS

Saving My Son

119 DAYS OF SMALL MIRACLES BEHIND THE NICU

ISBN: 978-1-7378345-4-0

Editor: Crystal S. Wright

10 9 8 7 6 5 4 3 2 1
Printed in the United States

Priceless Publishing®
Coral Springs, Fl
www.pricelesspublishing.co

Dedication

To Jaxson and Kamryn:

Because of you I believe in miracles.
May you always know that your lives are a
beautiful reflection of God's goodness and love.

Love,

Mommy

Contents

Introduction

I have endured and experienced a lot in my life - thankfully many highs but also many lows. Yet, one of the most pivotal and impactful parts of my journey has been that of becoming a Mother. With my firstborn, Jaxson, we had to fight to save his life after I unexpectedly went into preterm labor at 21 weeks. This book chronicles that journey which was my first NICU experience. God showed His sovereignty and demonstrated His omnipotence on this journey. I made a promise to Him that I would share what I've been through, and all of the miracles that I've been blessed to witness along the way.

I believe our scars can be the road map for someone else's journey. So I also wrote this book to spread awareness, and give hope to others who have experienced or are experiencing a tough motherhood journey. We don't just go through things for us, and my faith tells me that God does not waste anything. Everything serves a purpose, even the hard parts of life. May this book give you clarity on the purpose of your pain.

I candidly and transparently share our story because I know someone needs to hear it. I know that the journey of a Preemie Parent can feel lonely at times. Trust me, in the beginning we were lost in the sauce! Through this book, I want to establish a connection with other Preemie Parents, who may feel alone.

I want Parents who are in the thick of it to say *"if Ima made it, so can I."* I want my words to empower, encourage and uplift. I want you to read this book and know that miracles are real. May this book bless you and help you to believe the best even when things look impossible.

When you are forced to watch your Child fight for their life, you need an anchor to hold on to. For me, that's my faith in God. Without God, I really don't know where my family would be! I can say with confidence that He is still healing and working miracles. Having this confidence and conviction is freeing,. May your faith and hope be strengthened as you read my testimony.

Ima C.

PART I

When Pregnancy Leads To Emergency

The Baby Carriage

In Hebrew my name Ima, *(pronounced ee-ma)* means *Mother*. In Nigeria, which is where my Father is from, it means *love*. Ever since I was a little girl my dad called me Mommy J. He said I had this leadership quality and he always knew I would be a good Mother. I always found that to be endearing and prophetic in a way.

I've had a love for children for as long as I can remember. I always wanted to help in the nursery at church, and if I saw a Mom with her baby in church sitting nearby, I would always offer help. I was naturally drawn to children. I even had a love for playing with dolls, and playing house. It has just always been a deep desire inside of me to care for and nurture little ones. I grew up thinking about what kind of Mom I wanted to be. I remember playing little games like M.A.S.H where you write down your dreams and wishes on a piece of paper and fold it into an origami shape. It was so fun to see what *"my life"* would look like after manipulating the paper with my fingers.

I pictured myself being a stay-at-home mom to twins, or having kids and being my own boss running my own businesses. It's amazing how some of the things that we think about and long for when we are children find a way of coming to fruition. Around the age of about 11 or 12 years, I remember getting on my Mom's computer and creating business cards in Microsoft Word. I wanted to start my own babysitting service called *Little Diva's & Devo's*. I figured that I could do something I loved, while also making a little money. So, I had my business cards and I would pass them out at church and my Mom would also give them to people at her job.

Slowly but surely, my clientele grew. Word of mouth really helped me and I believe that I was able to learn so much during this time. I truly feel like each Family I worked for deposited nuggets of wisdom in me. The experiences of being a babysitter exposed me to different types of children and I held onto those experiences to use in my own motherhood journey.

I grew up in a nuclear, or 2 parent household until the age of 6, which is when my parents divorced. And though it was tough at times, I still held the dream in my heart to have a healthy marriage and build a beautiful family of my own. I never let my past take up pace for my future. I surrounded myself with positive examples, and constantly professed that my past doesn't define me. With time and lots of prayer, God blessed me with the desires of my heart.

In 2006, Marc and I went on our first date. We met through his younger sister and Mom who attended the same church I did. This was back in the MySpace and AOL days *(lol)*. As was customary then, we often chatted online and were just cool with each other. After our first date, I felt it was best to just remain friends.

There were some things I thought he needed to work on and the timing just didn't feel *right*. We stayed connected via social media and occasionally chatted with one another. Each year he would wish me a *Happy Birthday* on Facebook which I thought was just a nice gesture. I didn't think much more about it.

In the Summer of 2013 we were both single, and I was in a space where I was intentional about dating. The goal was marriage for me. Little did I know, he too was in the same mental space. So after innocently wishing him a *Happy Birthday* on Instagram, we exchanged a few comments and then he slid into my DMs! The conversation was organic and it led to us texting and then talking for hours. God's timing y'all!

Our love story was truly a beautiful whirlwind. We dated, fell in love and got married in a span of 22 months! Whew! From the start we had conversations about starting a family and building our lives together. My husband already had a child from a previous relationship which naturally brought some challenges to our relationship. But that did not deter us from wanting to create life together. Marc is such an amazing man and I already knew that he was a great Father. So, I figured that seeing him with the child we created together would be something special and magical.

FANTASY VS. REALITY

I think most women go into family planning not truly knowing what all it encompasses. I know for me, I was of the mindset that pregnancy would be blissful, easy and literally a walk in the park. Because why wouldn't it be? When you haven't experienced pregnancy, I think naturally there's a bit of naïveté. Society doesn't help with creating a false sense of sunshine and rainbows. I am not saying pregnancy isn't beautiful — it is — but there are so many unknowns.

The truth is, there can be lots of unexpected twists and turns. Although not every pregnancy or birth experience is traumatic, pregnancy is really life changing overall. Sharing your body with a little human requires a huge amount of sacrifice. You are literally creating everything that they need while also making sure you remain healthy, mentally, physically and otherwise.

But I believe that the miracle of life is beautiful and worth it all. My first pregnancy was unlike anything I could have ever imagined. There were no maternity photoshoots or baby shower, many long days spent in bed, sessions of hanging over the toilet and many trips to Urgent Care for fluids. It was hard. I think it's easy to sometimes get so caught up in our fantasy and ideals, that we neglect to take the time to appreciate the reality we have.

My journey to motherhood truly taught me so much about life and managing expectations. I gained an entire new perspective and appreciation for even the little things. I grew in my faith and became closer to my Husband. The rough journey also gave me the opportunity to experience miracles firsthand. What a privilege! Giving birth prematurely changed the trajectory of my life completely. What would've caused others to break, actually made ME stronger and empowered me to be the Woman I am today!

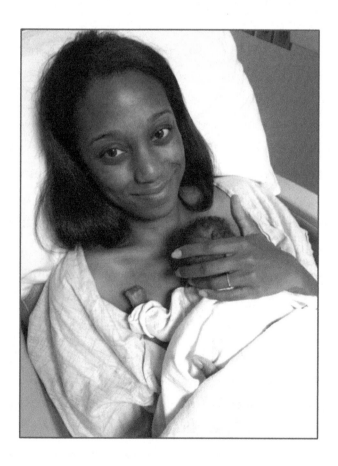

#Operation Keep Baby Baking

Ok, let me start at the beginning.

I found out that I was pregnant on a Friday morning. I was headed to work and just wasn't feeling well at all.

I remember being on the phone with my then fiancé and saying, *"Wow, the trash smells bad."*

I felt extremely dizzy too. It was rare for me to smell the trash so potently and strongly. It's been said that senses are heightened when you're pregnant. But honestly at that time, I wasn't thinking that I was pregnant but I definitely knew something was *off* with me. I ended up calling out of work because I felt it would be unsafe to drive across town feeling the way that I did. I took a pregnancy test and within seconds two pink lines popped up.

I was in shock! I honestly thought it was wrong and maybe just a fluke so I went to the CVS around the corner and got a 7-Up, crackers and an EPT test. I also quickly stopped at Dollar Tree to get another test. I needed to be sure! All 3 tests that I took read POSITIVE! I told Marc over the phone and we were both in a state of disbelief. Getting pregnant at the time that we did, was not the plan.

Later that day, I called around town to make a Doctor's appointment. I rested most of the day, but then my anxiety kicked in and I decided to go to Urgent Care which was about 10 minutes away for MORE testing.

There they took a urine sample, drew blood and asked a host of questions. I would have to wait until the following Wednesday *(Yes, Wednesday)* to get my results. Talk about torture! Yes, all of the urine tests came back positive, but I just felt like the blood draw would make things official OFFICIAL!

As the days went on I could hardly rest. You see, our wedding was just 9 weeks away! I still had to attend my bridal shower, bachelorette party, have the final dress fitting and do all the final preparations for the Big Day that we had been planning for 8 months.

Coming from a Christian background and home, pre-marital sex was a big fat NO NO! Getting pregnant *before* walking down the aisle was looked down upon, and I felt like the biggest hypocrite in the world. The guilt that I carried having "*known better*" was a lot. Marc and I had been in premarital counseling — which I highly recommend by the way — but it was required for us to be married by a Minister at our church. During this time our Counselors asked us and strongly encouraged us to abstain from sexual intercourse until our wedding. We worked really hard at doing so, but slipped up on Valentine's Day and got pregnant.

It took a lot of mental heavy lifting to push through the feelings that I was having in regards to being pregnant before marriage. Needless to say, we made it through the wedding and had a beautiful day. I kept my pregnancy a secret to the public until the middle of May which was after the wedding. I did not want the focus to be on being a pregnant Bride and having *those looks*. You know the looks I mean —those side eyes and awkward glances.

During this time and for the first time in my life, I was so sick to the point where I could hardly function. I felt like God was punishing me with horrible sickness because I had sinned. I know that sounds crazy but that's really how I felt. Morning sickness graduated to all-day-sickness around the 6 weeks. In the first trimester I developed a condition called Hyperemesis Gravidarum (HG), which is extreme nausea and vomiting that often leads to needing medical intervention.

This condition affects about 60,000 pregnant women per year and can be managed with medicine but is not completely preventable. I was unable to eat or drink pretty much anything without getting sick. My symptoms were so severe that I had to take a leave of absence from work. Urgent Care was becoming a very familiar place — I was there about twice a week to get treated for dehydration due to the daily excessive vomiting. I was losing weight due to not being able to eat and the fatigue was real. I started falling into depression — I was miserable. Here I was, a new wife and boss lady who couldn't do ANYTHING.

I would lay in bed and cry out to the Lord for mercy on me. The taste of water was unbearable. Drinking root beer with ice was really all I could tolerate. After back and forth trips to urgent care and to my OB, my symptoms were finally controlled with the help of a medication called Zofran, and at around 15/16 weeks I was starting to feel a bit better. I had to take my pill in the morning just to be able to function — I went from getting sick 8+ times a day to 1-2 times a day. I began to accept that this was my new reality.

To say that pregnancy was much different than I had imagined would be putting it lightly. I thought I was going to have a beautiful and fun pregnancy. I was looking forward to having a big round belly and being able to indulge in all of the delicious food I wanted, under the guise of *"cravings"*! But the first trimester had me laid out and the second trimester was cut short. As my HG started to get better, I was able to have some normalcy. I even started working again. By this time we had found out we were going to have a baby boy and Marc and I were ecstatic! We started discussing names and planning for our son. It was a welcome change to being sick and miserable.

We bought a home doppler so that we could listen to his heart beat in between ultrasounds. My baby was growing strong and healthy and I was starting to feel little flutters and his little kicks. Whenever I relaxed, I could see his little body ball up on one side of my belly. It was the most fascinating experience.

Finally, I was starting to enjoy having a precious miracle growing inside of me. I grew obsessed with Pinterest, and spent much time pinning for the baby shower, maternity photos, baby's nursery, clothes and just ALL things baby related!

Laying Down In Green Pastures

Out of the blue, I noticed that I started having vaginal irritation, so I went to see my OB. They told me I had a UTI which of course isn't uncommon for women to get, but in pregnancy this can cause complications if not treated efficiently. They prescribed 2 antibiotics and sent me on my way. Then I developed an allergy to one of the medications and was prescribed something else. Ok, no big deal.

About a week later, I was having a lot of discomfort, so much so that I called out of work and contacted my OB to discuss what was happening. I'm not sure if the switch in antibiotics caused the infection to get worse, but I ended up going in to be evaluated by one of the Drs. in the office as my OB was in with another patient.

I will never forget the look on her face as she performed my ultrasound. She had a look of confusion on her face. She left the room and came back with my OB and they checked me and the baby using a vaginal probe. These types of ultrasounds provide a much better look at the cervix and everything going on in the womb. It was then that I found out my cervix was beginning to dilate. I was 20-weeks pregnant and 1.6cm dilated. My OB told me to be calm and head straight to Labor & Delivery at the hospital.

Ok, wait, what? By this time I was in much pain, and scared. I called my Husband and my Mom and we all began to pray. I was admitted on July 9th for 24 hour observation and met with the high risk Doctor on call. His calm demeanor was comforting and unalarming which was greatly appreciated. I was given medication to stop the contractions and more antibiotics. Talk about things going from 0 to 100 pretty quickly. This officially started our mission of *#operationkeepbabybaking.*

During my 24-hour hospital stay and after several tests, I was discharged and allowed to be on home bed rest with restrictions. I was prescribed vaginal progesterone to be administered twice a day which was to help strengthen my cervix. I was also only allowed to get up to use the bathroom, and take a 10-minute shower every other day. These restrictions were put in place in order to alleviate any pressure on my cervix and not cause any more dilation.

With my husband working and me on leave again from work, I was literally confined to our master bedroom in our condo. There was only one window in our room and no AC. Did I mention it was July? Yea, it was brutal. Marc would prepare my breakfast, snacks and lunch and put it in a cooler on ice for me, accompanied by a food tray. During this time, I rested, prayed, watched TV, read and just stayed still. I wasn't sure what God was trying tell me during this time. I went from being an on-the-go woman to literally laying down in green pastures as the Lord restored my soul.

DR. GOOGLE: A BLESSING AND A CURSE

Over the course of 4 days of being on bed rest, I started to embrace my current situation. Each day I remained pregnant was a blessing and I was grateful to keep my baby baking. On July 14th I noticed a slight pink discharge but didn't think too much of it. I was also experiencing a lot of pressure and what felt like cramps. The discomfort lasted all day and night and wouldn't let up. I went on Google to self-diagnose — I am sure we all know how Google can be a gift and a curse. Dr. Google had me confused lol.

I called Labor & Delivery and spoke to a nurse in triage. She told me to drink a lot of water, take a warm bath and if I didn't feel better then I should come in to be on the safe side. Around midnight after trying to go to sleep and having tears in my eyes, I asked my husband to take me to the hospital. The pain was at a level 8 *(on a scale of 1 to 10 with 10 being unbearable)*, and my Mama instinct told me something wasn't right. I was so scared of what was happening and what my diagnosis would be. But I knew I needed to get checked. The triage nurse that I had spoken to over the phone would also be the one to take care of me, my Angel Julie.

An ultrasound technician came and performed a few different tests. I was under the impression that maybe these were just Braxton Hicks and we would go back home shortly and continue bed rest. More time passed and at this point it had to have been around 3am. My nurse, Julie, came in with this look of despair on her face.

I asked her if I was going to be able to go home soon and she said, *"I'm sorry, Sweetie but you have dilated more and are having contractions."*

That explained the pain and discomfort that I was having.

The tears immediately started streaming down my face. I was devastated. Through salty tears and a crackling voice I begged for answers that she wasn't supposed to give. She told me I was 8.2cm dilated. I lost it even more. Marc who had been strong for the both of us began to cry. Julie rushed to me and gave me a hug and cried with me. Once I calmed down a bit, Marc left the room to call his parents and my mom. I would later find out that he collapsed on the floor telling his parents the news. My mom and in-laws rushed to the hospital as we had no idea of what was to come.

As I was being admitted, Julie came back to tell me that she had made a mistake and I was actually 2.8cm dilated NOT 8.2cm — what a relief. But still, our hope was still hanging in the balance. It wasn't making sense how I was getting worse yet had been doing all of the right things. I was officially 22 weeks and 3 days pregnant.

Over the next several hours we would be inundated with information from the NICU team and my OB. Our hearts were breaking with each person that spoke to us. I laid in bed crying and fearful as my husband broke down too with our parents at our side. Being broken is an interesting state to be in. Brokenness brings a vulnerability that is so palpable that everyone near you can feel it.

At the time I didn't realize that God was breaking us, not to tear us down, but to build us back up.

Save My Son!

We were forced to make decisions that no parent should be faced with. The options were presented with different outcomes and we didn't have a long time to decide. My OB suggested we go with *"comfort care"*, which means to *"let nature take its course."* If I were to go into full on labor, there would be no intervention, and no resuscitation for the baby. His reason for suggesting this was because of the gestation of our son and possible developmental issues. His words were chilling to the core as he candidly suggested that we, *"try again in the future"* since we were young. Yep, he actually said those words!

One could only assume the many health challenges that our unborn son would have due to his early birth. But we had reached the midway point of pregnancy so the decision to just give up on him wasn't so cut and dry. At the time I was technically 22 weeks, 3 days but he was measuring ahead by a few days. The goal was to make it to at least 24 weeks, they said the baby would have a better chance.

My husband and I went back and forth for a while discussing our options. Would it be comfort care, which meant allowing him to come into the world on his own but not receive life-saving measures? Or, did we want to take an aggressive approach to stop labor which ultimately meant giving our son more time to grow and develop in my womb? We prayed, cried, discussed the options, then cried some more.

My OB came back in the room to find out what we wanted to do and I looked him in the eyes with tears streaming down my face, and I told him, *"Save my son! I don't care what happens to me, just save him and give him a chance."*

At that moment I truly felt like a Mother — an Advocate. I was fighting for someone I had yet to meet but knew deserved a chance. From that point forward the aggressive approach began and I was given antibiotics to build my immune system up in case any more infections were to arise: a magnesium drip to stop labor, surfactant to protect my baby's brain and Betamethasone steroid shots to help my baby's lungs. This is a normal course of treatment when a mother faces premature labor.

The first round of magnesium produced the worst side effects. I was told that I may hallucinate, become nauseous, vomit and experience hot flashes. Within moments of the medicine flowing through my veins, I felt not one, but ALL of the side effects at the same time. My mother-in-law was fanning me as my husband held my hand and my mom stood close by praying. I didn't realize saving my baby would be so hard mentally and physically to the point where it would literally send my body into a state of shock.

Over the next few days both myself and the baby were stable. The plan was to remain on hospital bedrest. Our first goal was to make it to 24 weeks which is deemed as most viable. The bigger goal was to remain pregnant at least until 32-34 weeks. My family and I stayed in prayer and made the best of our situation. We celebrated each day that I stayed pregnant because it was a blessing and a milestone. During this time of stillness, I spent a lot of time talking to God, napped and kept my spirits high as much as possible.

Being completely helpless is such a humbling experience. I never expected to go through anything like this while pregnant. I had to rely on my faith, my medical team and my family. And it became uncomfortable physically and emotionally after only a few days. Having no control of the situation and having to rely on others was something I definitely was not used to. But I knew this is where we needed to be, and keeping that at the forefront of my mind gave me some peace so I could keep a positive outlook.

Although I was a bit scared, I knew making the decision to fight for my boy was the right decision. I trusted in the Lord more than I ever have in my life. After all, He knew ahead of time what would happen. Knowing that our present circumstance wasn't a shock to God allowed me to keep a calm disposition about everything. I knew no matter the outcome, we would make it through.

At 4:30am on Saturday, July 18, 2015 I frantically woke up to discomfort in my pelvic area. This was a very distinct feeling accompanied by what looked like dry blood in my bed. I felt very strong pressure and the feeling of needing to use the restroom. I carefully tried to get out of bed and head to the bathroom all the while paging my nurse, Carla. I wasn't able to reach her by pressing the button so I called on the phone and said I needed a nurse ASAP.

I will never forget the look on Carla's face as she rushed into the room to check on me. She told me to get back in the bed and trying to lighten the mood I cleverly replied, *"Why, is my baby going to fall out?"*

She looked at me with a stoic look and said, *"I don't know, so let's get you back in bed."*

You see Carla had been my nurse for 2 nights and we had formed a bond. This was the first time I had seen her seriously concerned. The night before all of this I was in such good condition that I encouraged my husband to go home and get a good night's rest. He had been sleeping in the hospital room with me every night.

Of course, the night that I sent him home is the night that all of the action started taking place. He truly took my advice and was getting such a good night's sleep that he did not hear the phone.

I was calling to let him know that I was in preterm labor again and that he needed to get to the hospital right away. I called my mom as well and she wasn't answering the phone either.

I couldn't believe that everyone was in this deep sleep. I needed them to be by my side ASAP. I was scared and shocked at how rapidly my condition changed. I'm not sure how much time passed, but I eventually made contact and Marc arrived to be by my side. Over the next several hours the atmosphere in my room quickly changed as the NICU team started making preparations. I was given a host of medication to yet again, stop my very active labor.

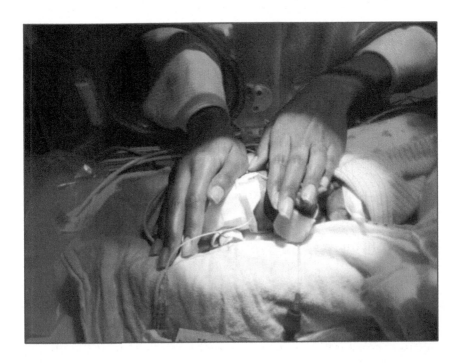

READY OR NOT, HERE I COME!

The night shift ended at 7:30am meaning my favorite nurse Carla would be leaving me in the hands of another nurse. I'll be honest, that made me nervous and my family spoke with the Charge Nurse to make sure I was assigned to a nurse that was already familiar with my case. Thankfully, Jenna, who was my nurse when I had to undergo 24-hour monitoring, was working that day and she was assigned to me. She labored with me, held my hand and truly just comforted me during such an emotional day.

The medication I was given caused my labor to slow down. However, it didn't completely stop it and that meant my son would definitely be born on July 18th! I endured 10 hours of excruciating pain — a pain I never knew before, and now will never forget. The contractions were happening so fast and so strong it literally took my breath away. I had previously spoken with my OB about performing a C-Section in order to give my son the best chance at surviving. Giving birth vaginally was likely to have caused him to go into distress and possibly not make it.

Throughout my laboring, he had a strong and steady heartbeat which I'm thankful for. It gave me confirmation that we were doing the right thing, though very tough and painful. By the 10th hour the team wanted to check and see how dilated I was but that wasn't possible because my bag was bulging and Baby Boy was sitting low

— hence, the fluid that had been leaking since 4:30am. In reality, I was probably ready to push, but for some reason they held off and let me labor. Every extra minute inside my womb was necessary for my baby's health and survival.

I finally asked for an epidural because the pain was becoming quite unbearable. Once the anesthesiologist arrived to give me the epidural, I felt a bit at ease knowing relief was on the way. Getting an epidural was never in my birth plan, but as you now know, nothing from my birth plan went as planned. Yes, I was terrified of the needle but I was more exhausted. I knew I needed some extra support to help me through the process.

A few short minutes after getting the epidural, I was hooked up to the fetal monitor as Jenna was having a little trouble finding his heartbeat. You see, what happened was my son had flipped over into breech position and had become tachycardic. The monitors started going off and the concern for me and the baby got serious. Everything went from a 2 to a 10 in a matter of seconds.

My room was filled with nurses and doctors. A catheter was quickly inserted inside of me and I was whisked away for an emergency c-section. My body was going into shock as the medical team rushed me down the hallway and my husband quickly followed while putting on his scrubs. I vividly remember a woman asking me if I consented to have a c-section (because things were happening so fast I didn't have a chance to sign documents ahead of time).

I told the woman, *"Yes, give me the c-section, just SAVE MY SON!"*

She then proceeded to ask me, *"Are you sure?"*

I yelled, *"YES!!!!!!"*

I was literally on the operating table getting prepped while having this conversation. I still shake my head thinking about that particular moment when they were about to cut me open. Over the next 20 minutes, I would go in and out of awareness. I was heavily medicated but awake. I felt every tug on my abdomen and the pressure was very painful. In hindsight, I wish I could have been asleep for the procedure because it was a bit traumatic.

I remember asking my husband if the baby was out, and telling him to leave me and go be with our son. At this point, I was in a state of shock where I was lucid but shaking. I was told that I lost a lot of blood — not enough to need to be transfused, but a lot nonetheless. My husband left with the NICU team as they rushed my 1lb 2.9oz baby away to save his life.

I laid on that table alone, scared and delirious saying things like, *"I want to eat BBQ now that I've had the baby."*

I asked for my OB because he wasn't there when I was first brought into the operating room. Thankfully, he made it back in time to help stitch me up, as the other doctors congratulated me on doing a good job. During my operation, my OB revealed that I had 5 fibroids. This was new information, as I had gone 30 years of my life being healthy and even having normal periods since the age of 12. It made me wonder if this could've caused some of my pregnancy complications.

Nevertheless, once I was stitched up Nurses wheeled me to the recovery room and I fell into a deep sleep. I was soooo out of it, but I heard voices and people moving around me, and shivered from the cold air in the room. I would stay in recovery for a couple hours before being taken to my new room.

PART II

Welcome To
Preemie Parenthood

Going Home Without My Baby

Not many understand the emotional burden that parents deal with when it comes to leaving their baby in the NICU. There was no manual for it, and not many people talk about it. For days, weeks and months it felt like we were living on edge. One day could be great and then the next everything could change. Our brains were constantly in learning mode, soaking up medical terms and numbers nonstop! There was no time to curl up in bed and be sad. Nope. I was pumping breastmilk around the clock, going back and forth to the hospital and trying to create some sort of balance.

One of Jaxson's Doctors always encouraged my husband and I to spend time together and do fun things. The first couple of months were hard because I was still recovering from my c-section and Jaxson was still medically fragile. We spent time together by Jaxson's bedside and it made us happy and comfortable so to speak. Being by his side was our new normal.

Prior to having Jaxson, I wasn't fond of hospitals so it was interesting to me that I found comfort in a place that used to freak me out. I think the peace of mind came from just being present and not having to worry about the hospital calling us with an emergency because we were right there!

Let me tell you, I had a lot of anxiety going to bed many nights. Although Jaxson was pretty stable after the first couple of months, going to bed was still sometimes the hardest thing for me. NICU Parents often fear getting a phone call from the Hospital. Hearing my phone vibrate in the middle of the night from a text message or email would startle me.

Thankfully, we never received any of those middle-of-the-night phone calls saying we needed to get back to the hospital immediately. So many parents are experiencing the NICU for the first time and trying to process their new normal. Being sad, afraid, anxious, stressed, unsure, etc. IS NORMAL! If you are feeling any of these things, you are not crazy.

MAINTAINING BALANCE

Are people telling you that you are overreacting? Has someone told you to stop being so sad? Do you feel like no one understands? I encourage you to clearly tell and describe to your Family and Friends the kind of support you need from them. If you don't feel like talking or want visitors, let them know in a nice way.

If you need help, be honest about it. If you just need someone to listen to you vent, there are great support groups on social media and maybe even at your hospital, with other parents who will completely understand what you are going through.

And for the strangers and coworkers who may say something crazy, it's ok to correct them and let them know they need to mind their own business :).

Do you feel like you need a break from the NICU? Is hospital life consuming you? Or do you feel like you need to be there 24/7?

I think it's really up to you and your Family to create a schedule that works best. For the first couple of weeks of our NICU journey, we were winging it and would spend countless hours in Jaxson's room just watching him, talking or I would pump breastmilk. As time went on, we developed a bit of a schedule with our visits and would go before his touch times to help with his cares, and hold him until his next touch time.

Some may not agree with me but I knew sitting by my son's bedside for 24 hours wasn't healthy for me. I was constantly staring at the monitor and oftentimes unable to relax. Also, Jaxson could sense our presence and would become a little restless for whatever reason and not be able to rest like he needed to. As time went on, we really found our groove and a balance that worked well for our Family.

So, my advice is to create a schedule and a routine that works for you. This is the best way to navigate during this journey. If your schedule allows, go at the times you know your baby will be awake and at the time when you can participate in their cares (diaper change, feeding, temperature check, etc). Know that it is OK to take a day of rest if you need to. The back-and-forth trips can be draining. It's ok to call throughout the day and check in if you aren't going. Please don't let the guilt of not going for a visit consume you.

Being in the NICU is a world of its own. You can easily lose track of time and get totally consumed. I encourage you to take breaks, go outside and get some air. Have lunch away from the hospital. Take a walk. Take a nap. Prepare for your baby to come by nesting. Having creative projects kept me occupied *outside* of the NICU! And remember, you cannot pour from an empty cup! So, make sure to fill yours from time to time!

Bonding Beyond The Incubator

Bonding with your baby during this time is very important. While being in the NICU is not the ideal situation, it is still crucial that you do all you can to connect with your baby. Think about it. They are surrounded by strangers all day, so your presence is important. I know some parents struggle with feeling like their baby doesn't know who they are. That's an absolutely normal feeling. But believe it or not, babies know when their parents are near. The bond between Mom/Dad and baby is so unique and special. Jaxson knew our voices and would do little things to show us that he recognizes his Mommy and Daddy.

I remember during the first few weeks I was so afraid to touch him. His skin was gelatinous and he was very fragile. I didn't want to hurt him by touching him. I didn't want to get too close to him. I was afraid…afraid of losing him, and truly in shock about what was happening. So, I kept my distance. His amazing nurses encouraged me to gently rest my hands on his tiny frame to assure me that I wouldn't hurt him.

Upon entering the NICU, visitors are required to thoroughly scrub their hands, nails and arms for several minutes in the washroom. I timidly stuck my hands through the 2 small holes on his incubator and did what's called the *containment hold*. From that moment on I felt a connection like never before. But I was still afraid of getting too close.

You see, when your child is given a 20% percent chance of surviving, it causes an array of emotions. The first emotion I had was fear of getting too attached. I had no idea what to expect — I was in somewhat of a fog. I didn't get to hold him on my chest immediately following his birth, so I felt that he wouldn't know who I was, but I was wrong.

In the moments when he was a little agitated from the lights, sounds and wires, I would rest my hands on him and he would instantly calm down. His vitals would stabilize and I knew he felt comforted by his Mama. I wasn't able to hold him until he was 28 days old. Dad held him for the first time at 32 days old. Prior to that, day in and day out we visited the NICU and all we could do was touch his tiny hands and his itty-bitty toes. It was hard. But I knew our presence was a blessing to him. Even sitting bedside and praying for him and watching him sleep was special and helped us stay connected.

I had to find ways to bond with him despite him being in his incubator. I had to look past the equipment and the wires and the tubes down his throat. I had to block out the beeping noises from the machines. I had to fight through the emotions of feeling guilty and helpless. Jaxson's touch times were every 3 hours — that's when we would help with his cares: diaper changes, taking his temperature, helping with his baths and preparing my breast milk for his tube feeds. Doing these things helped me feel like his Mom and not just a visitor.

There truly is a sacredness that comes from being a Preemie Parent and watching your baby fight through the NICU. Though there are so many hard moments, there are also really beautiful ones as well — moments where you just feel this indescribable connection that can't be broken. We were his peace and calm — his safe place and I felt that.

I wrote this poem one day while at my son's bedside.

For a while there weren't many things that I could do,
So I would just stand there and look at you.

Carefully memorizing your every move,
your perfect little toes, and beautiful baby hair.

Yep, I was that stalker Mom who stared.

Sometimes your nurses would ask me if I wanted a seat
And I would think, "No, I have the perfect view here"
Just watching you sleep.

You were so tiny but so strong.
I had yet to hold you in my arms.

My heart loved you, and ached
for that special touch of your skin on mine.

My mind would sometimes race —
This was our new reality staring us right in the face.

We fought for 5 1/2 months together…
I enjoyed your every move.

Your little kicks were perfect when you were growing safely inside me.
Wow, that was perfect!

Although our birth story wasn't the way your dad and I planned,
It was certainly God's perfect plan.

After each visit my heart would get a little more full.
This mother and son bond was in full bloom.

We were bonding beyond the incubator.
Though the days and nights are often long,

I'm enjoying watching you grow strong.
Daddy's little fighter and Mommy's perfect miracle.

You formed in my womb and I watched you develop.
Our hearts are connected.

We have created a bond that can never be broken,
A bond that will last forever....

Little Miracles

In the NICU there's a specific time period that's considered *The Honeymoon Period*. This usually occurs within the first 7 days of life. Our first 7 days were smooth and relatively peaceful, especially considering we had a 22-weeker who was given a 20% chance of surviving. One of the doctors told my Husband that the first 24 hours would be extremely critical. And although he was critical by definition, we are incredibly blessed with how much of fight he had. Each day Jaxson was stable and surviving was a miracle. Some of the Nurses and RTs would express their surprise for how well he was doing. Again, we knew this was a miracle and that God was doing just what He said He would do — saving our precious boy.

Suddenly, when Jaxson was 9-days-old he started declining and required the maximum amount of oxygen support. His fragile and underdeveloped lungs were filling with fluid and it was a huge cause for concern. Essentially, this was being caused by a PDA (Patent ductus arteriosus — a persistent opening between the two major blood vessels leading from the heart). This is a common issue for micro Preemies.

The opening (ductus arteriosus), is a normal part of a baby's circulatory system in the womb that usually closes shortly after birth. But due to preterm birth, those vessels don't fully develop and this can lead to complications. He had been on medication to treat his PDA, but his body was not responding to it. This was scary and a shock after having a pretty decent week.

Marc and I had a care conference with the NICU team that morning upon arriving at the NICU. I'll never forget that feeling or the look on the Doctor's face. I was finally warming up to being a Mom to a Preemie. I had let my guard down and allowed myself to connect to my baby. I was slowly coming out of my traumatic birth fog. And BOOM, we get the news that he isn't doing well, and we have to make some important decisions.

I was crushed to my core. We were pulled into a cold tiny room with stark faces looking at us and telling us that my Jaxson would need surgery ASAP in order to save his life. I broke down in tears and was nearly inconsolable. I remember wondering, how did we get here? I thought we were out of the woods. Marc stayed strong for us while I had my moment. We were forewarned that the NICU would be a roller coaster, but we didn't anticipate things escalating so quickly, and it completely took me by surprise.

Operating on our son sounded like it was the best and only option to save his life. We had come too far to turn around and because there was a CHANCE, we simply had to take it. But there were so many things that had to be considered first! He would have to be transferred to a Children's Hospital across town during rush hour traffic. Talk about nerves, if you know anything about California then you know it can take an hour to go 20 miles.

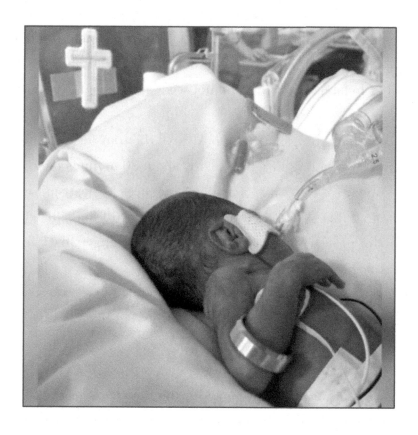

AN EMERGENCY OPERATION

The first step in the process of having him transferred was for him to undergo a head ultrasound. This would determine if he had a brain bleed. If he did have one then they would have considered him not stable enough to be transferred. For reference, bleeds usually show up in the first few days. So, while they performed the test, Marc and I went across the street to take a breath, try and eat, pray and let our Village know what was going on so that they could be in prayer too. The head ultrasound was performed and they called us to let us know they did not see a brain bleed.

From there things moved quickly and the transfer team was on their way from Long Beach (which is about 30 minutes or so from the hospital we were at). I was doing my best to stay calm in the midst of all this. When the transfer team arrived I immediately felt a sense of peace come over me. There was a younger Black female Neonatologist who approached us, and went over what was about to take place. Her demeanor was very peaceful — she was calm yet confident that our son would be ok. I truly felt like God had sent her to us.

As Jaxson was being prepped for the transfer, small talk led to us sharing our faith with her and how we believed that Jaxson was a miracle. She told us she too was a believer. At that moment I was amazed that God would use this Doctor to bless us and show us that He truly is concerned about all things concerning our son.

She asked if she could pray with us, and my heart was overflowing with gratitude. This interaction in itself was a miracle. You don't usually come across medical professionals who will share their faith and match it with yours.

No shade, but leading up to that moment, every Doctor we had dealt with would just look at us funny when we expressed how much of a miracle Jaxson was. There were a couple of the Doctors that told us straight to our faces that they believe in science and they don't believe in miracles. That was tough to hear. So, as a woman of faith who was wholeheartedly relying on God to perform a miracle for her son, having someone who was caring for him believe what we were believing provided such peace.

When Jaxson was all ready to go, we kissed his little face and they loaded him up in the ambulance to transfer him across town. About an hour later he arrived at the hospital and they got him settled into his new space. The new hospital was much different than what we had become used to. Unlike having a private and quiet room at his birth hospital, the new NICU had about 10 critical babies in one big room partitioned off into pods.

If I sit still long enough I can still hear the chimes and bells from all of the different machines. This NICU was much more active and overwhelming. It lacked the level of privacy we had quickly grown accustomed to. But it's where our son needed to be so we got with the program! The hospital was also a teaching hospital and they rotated teams every week. That in itself was a little nerve wracking just knowing there would be so many different people involved in our son's care.

On the first night there was a little bit of a clash with one of the Neonatologists on call. Once Jaxson was settled into his pod, we went in to see him and the Doctor badgered me with questions. It was like rapid fire style. He didn't believe that Jaxson was a 22-weeker and tried to gaslight me. It was unsettling and actually brought me to tears. He suggested that I didn't have my dates correct for my cycle. He couldn't believe that the birth hospital resuscitated Jaxson 3 times and that he survived. He was dumbfounded that Jaxson looked as well as he did. This was the Doctor's first interaction with a 22-week Preemie.

I stood by the truth with tears in my eyes. Thankfully our Angel Doctor stepped in and took us under her wing. She again comforted us while still doing her job, and let us know she would help us all get through this. The following day we met with the most amazing Cardiologist who reviewed Jaxson's case and felt positive about performing the surgery. Jaxson was only about 1lb 3 oz. at the time. He was still very small, but boy was he a fighter!

Thanks to Marc, we had people all over the world praying for Jaxson and fully invested in our journey at this time. He had taken it upon himself on the day Jaxson was born to start sharing our journey on social media. The prayers and support really carried us through and I remained confident that Jaxson would make it through his surgery.

And pull through he did, with flying colors. It was a miracle how well he was recovering. The team of Neonatologists had a much more aggressive approach of care. Thankfully, our Doctor of Faith had our backs and really held our hands through the ups and downs of those first few weeks of NICU life.

A few days following Jaxson's PDA surgery, they performed another head ultrasound and saw that he had a grade 1 brain bleed. On one hand we were terrified and then on the other thankful for the miracle within that. Remember I told you that if a bleed would have shown up prior to him being transferred, they wouldn't have done it. God was working behind the scenes and covering our boy, I just knew it.

Some people look at things like this as luck or a coincidence. And no offense if that's your thing, but I believe in the power of God. I believe that God goes before us and leads us. I believe He knows what's lying ahead before we get even there. I believe that He cares deeply for us and doesn't want to harm us. He doesn't give us too much to knock us off our feet, and provides grace to sustain us.

Without a shadow of a doubt, over the 3 weeks that Jaxson was at the NICU where he had surgery, God was performing small yet impactful miracles. Having an emergency operation on day 13 of life, learning all we needed to know from our Doctor of Faith and trusting their plan of care to give him the DART protocol (steroids) to help his lungs was a game changer.

Interventions like this are so critical early on. Yes, it was more of an aggressive approach, but Jaxson proved that he could handle it. He didn't have any setbacks. He actually propelled forward and by day 27, he was able to be extubated (taken off the ventilator) and put on CPAP bubble.

Being off the vent meant that he could now be held by me and Dad. On day 28, Jaxson was having such a good and stable day that his Nurses finally gave me a chance to do kangaroo care with him. I still remember this day so vividly. It was my first time holding my first-born and I was elated and a little nervous. Two nurses helped transfer Jaxson from his incubator and placed him on my chest.

Marc beamed with pride as he captured this special moment on video and camera. Having Jaxson so close to my heart was perfect. His oxygen saturation levels were high and he required less oxygen support. His heart rate showed that he was relaxed. For the first 27 days Jaxson's life, we didn't hear his voice because he had a tube down his throat. But he made the cutest little squeals and grunts, and they were truly music to our ears.

After a few more days at the hospital we had transferred to, Jaxson was stable enough to go back to his birth hospital. Yes, he had a brain bleed, but it was self-resolving so the Team didn't have concerns that the transfer would negatively affect him. He was also 4 weeks old (26 weeks gestation) at this time. Once he made it back Marc and I felt so much stronger than when he had left.

We learned SO much and were able to take that knowledge and empowerment with us. It's as if God refined us while we were in that fire. We didn't get burned but rather we came out pure as gold. From then on, day by day we saw miracles happening with our son. According to the statistics, he was doing better than what was predicted. That's what makes him such a miracle.

For a baby born so early, we were told there was a high probability of Jaxson having countless issues, such as not being able to walk, talk or live a full thriving life. We never accepted that. We believed God would do the extraordinary. This is not to say we would've loved our son any less if things went a different way.

I'm just saying that we strongly believed that God was going to perform a miracle. And let me tell you, people will think you are crazy until that CRAZY thing you are believing happens.

Faith & Fight

During the short time of being at home and on bed rest I started to wrap my mind around what was happening. I hadn't had a chance to pack a hospital bag, take maternity photos, pick a solid name, tour the hospital, do prenatal yoga, get a 3d/4d ultrasound, have our baby shower or take a parenting class! I held onto my hope and my faith during these moments thinking God surely must have a plan.

I constantly told myself that there must be a blessing awaiting us on the other side of this storm. Not too much time later, God began to show me that He wanted us to experience a real-life MIRACLE. Not just a miracle that you hear about through a third party, but one that was our own and one that would touch lives near and far.

In May 2015 at just 3 months pregnant, I was lying in bed (sooo sick from having HG) listening to a sermon from Bishop Neil Ellis. He said something that was so deep that at the time didn't really click. He said and I quote:

"In the next 9 months expect an off season miracle. God is getting ready to speed things up!"

I was so sick in bed watching this and just taking in the words not fully grasping what that meant for me. But I held those words in my heart. It wasn't until Jaxson was about 2 weeks old that it hit me — Jaxson was my off-season miracle! He wasn't expected to be born until November 2015. The sermon was preached in February 2015 the same month Jaxson was conceived. That's 9 months! Everything started to really make sense to me then. God was performing a miracle right before our eyes for all to see!

Going through this was going to test my faith like never before. I know many people believe in good luck or good fortune but as for me I truly believe in the power of God and how He shows up in our lives. I grew up in church and always had faith. My Mom made sure I knew who God was and helped to instill godly principles in my life. But it's not until you go through things personally and begin to trust God in the midst of your own experiences, that you really see how good and sovereign He is.

This NICU journey we were on is what God used to bring us closer to Him, and even to one another as a couple. I got to experience God in a way that I've only heard about. I've read the Bible and I really believe that He turned water into wine. He raised the dead. He is able to do all that He says He can do! That's the kind of faith I had to develop in order to really make it day by day in the NICU.

I am human so some days I had to fight my flesh and really believe boldly that God would do exactly what we prayed for. I am well aware that He is no genie in a bottle. But I firmly believe that when we are in HIS will, He will give us the desires of our heart and bless us.

Faith is behaving like what God told you is the truth! Faith is the substance of things hoped for, the evidence of things unseen. I can say wholeheartedly that we wouldn't have made it through without God. When I felt like I couldn't press on one more day, one more hour, or even one more minute, I held onto my faith and my hope. It sustained me. It strengthened me. Life as a new mom let alone a NICU parent to a micro-Preemie will test your faith like never before.

My husband and I would pray prayers that we had never even thought we would utter. We were putting our faith to work even when we couldn't see our way through the storm. We now had the great responsibility to fight for our family. That meant fighting off negative thoughts and focusing on the positive every day, even on the hard days. Every day Jaxson made it through was a victory. Every day I was able to pump milk and give him the nutrients he needed was a miracle. Every day we saw the hand of God and His protection over Jaxson.

"Marvelous are Your works, and that my soul knows very well."
— Psalm 139:14

I will never forget a few Preemie moms telling us to celebrate the good days because they will help us get through the not-so-good ones. Because when your baby is in the NICU it often feels like you are taking 2 steps forward and 4 backwards. It's an exhausting dance. And some days I had to fight through hard emotions and feelings in order to fight for my son. My husband and I were his advocates, which meant sometimes having hard conversations with the nurses and doctors. The days were long and the nights were even longer, but we labored in love daily.

You may be going through a fight of your own, be it a health challenge, relationship or marital issue, dysfunction on the job, etc. I want to encourage you to dig deep within yourself and pull out the fight that's within you. You have the courage and power in you to fight through whatever hardship you may be faced with. Sometimes when life hits us hard, we just want to hide under the covers and hope the issue resolves itself. Even when I wanted to do that, I knew I couldn't stay in that place. If you have to cry your way through, that's ok. Just don't stay stuck in that place. Pick up those pieces of defeat and use them to stay in the race and finish strong. Remember that your labor is not in vain.

"Let us not become weary in doing good, for at the proper time we will reap a harvest if we do not give up."
— Galatians 6:9

When Jaxson was just 3 months old, he had to undergo a procedure on his right eye. Around 32 weeks gestation he began to develop ROP (Retinopathy of Prematurity) which in severe cases if left untreated can cause blindness. During his first eye exam, the ophthalmologist said everything looked fine and she would reexamine in 2 weeks. Within that time frame Jaxson's eye development quickly deteriorated. The part of the eye that ROP affects is the retina. By stage 4 the retina is likely detached from the eyeball and blindness occurs. Within 2 weeks, Jaxson had developed Stage 2, Zone 1 ROP in both eyes.

He initially had weekly eye exams, but once the deterioration began he had to have his eyes examined twice a week in the NICU. And remember I mentioned the 2 steps forward and 4 steps backwards feeling? Well, as the left eye stayed stable, the right eye got worse (Stage 2, Zone 2). Jaxson needed emergency surgery the following day. I was shaken by the news. This would be his second surgery while in the NICU.

I had a work meeting following that phone call and I was visibly not ok, but tried to push through. I left work and met Marc at our son's bedside. I just wanted to give him some extra cuddles and pray over him. I knew what was ahead could be tough on him. He had to be intubated again and put on the ventilator which he hadn't been on since he was just a few weeks old. He also had to be sedated because the surgery required him to be completely still.

The Doctor did an Avastin injection which is a treatment that destroys the damaged tissue and allows new tissue to develop. The surgery was successful, however the recovery process took 3 days.

The sedation medication made it very hard for Jaxson to wake up and breathe on his own. While his eye was in much better shape, he began having respiratory issues. Issues that he never had. We were devastated. It felt like all of the progress Jaxson had made had been thrown out the window. The longer he remained intubated, the harder it would be for him to come off.

We fervently prayed for a miracle. The same God who had saved our son in the very beginning could do it again. I believed that wholeheartedly, even though he was now the sickest baby on the NICU floor. I couldn't believe how quickly things had changed. My faith was being tested. I didn't understand why after 3 months this was happening.

His oxygen settings were maxed out at 100%. One of his lungs collapsed and he had a touch of pneumonia. He was given antibiotics and they told us he just needed time to get stronger to come out of this. Those 3 days were very hard and sad for us. We never lost hope that our son would pull through, but it was definitely scary watching him fight, and feeling like there wasn't much we could do. There was one thing I could do for Jaxson though, and that was pray. I did what I knew best and trusted God with the rest. During this time our Doctor of Faith came by to see him as well, which was comforting.

And on the third day, he was back! Dare I say, he was better than before! He was able to be extubated and put on high flow oxygen with low settings. In those 3 days God was working on Jaxson behind the scenes. He was able to rest and let the machines do what needed to be done so he could come back stronger than ever. It was a miracle we didn't even see coming, but so grateful for!

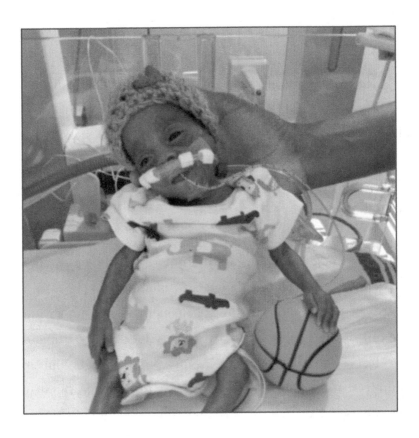

Super Dad

You know how some say men express their emotions differently than women? Well, it's true! And because of that, sometimes it can lead to friction and even drifting apart in a relationship. Crisis and trauma can be huge triggers. If there's a lack of understanding and good communication, navigating through times will be even harder. And I would say from my experience that watching your baby fight for their lives is one of the hardest life experiences.

For us, this journey came in the midst of us being newlyweds. So, we were navigating our new life together while simultaneously having this huge thing happen to our Family. Overnight, we became advocates and had to be on one accord. When I was down, my Husband was the strong one, encouraging me, speaking up for us and making sure we were good. When he was down, I took the lead. I let him have his moment and never shamed him for it. A part of navigating such a traumatic and life-changing experience is to truly take things one step at a time. Lean on one another, ask the questions and don't just assume.

In the beginning of our NICU journey I wasn't fully in a space to talk openly about what was going on. I was in a state of shock and so many things were happening fast. Marc took it upon himself to share what we were going through on Facebook. From the moment he posted that I was going in for an emergency c-section and asked for prayer, sooooo many people became invested in our journey.

He then began giving updates on my and Jaxson's condition. As a Preemie Father who was standing by, he felt a bit helpless. So, asking for prayers and sharing in this way really helped him express and process what was going on. He was transparent and candid in a way that was so beautiful. He turned into our Family Photographer.

Seeing Jaxson through his eyes is still so special to me. Every picture he captured tells such a timeless story and each time someone sees a glimpse of Jaxson's journey, they are moved by it. Instead of Marc withdrawing due to his own sadness, fears and thoughts, he leaned in and became a Super Dad. Whenever I tell people that he is the one who created Jaxson's Instagram page they are always so impressed. I let him have that space and truly appreciate him taking that on and allowing me to contribute as I feel comfortable. I also appreciate that he willingly stepped into that position.

I consider myself extremely blessed to have such an amazing and supportive Husband. Recovering from my c-section and learning to pump my breastmilk was hard! He was right by my side every day and was so very helpful. I mean literally helping me to the bathroom and holding me when I could barely walk. Even the Nurses were impressed with him and expressed how helpful he was. So much so that they told him he would have a great career as a nurse! Marc is really good with people and the way he loves and protects our Family is a blessing.

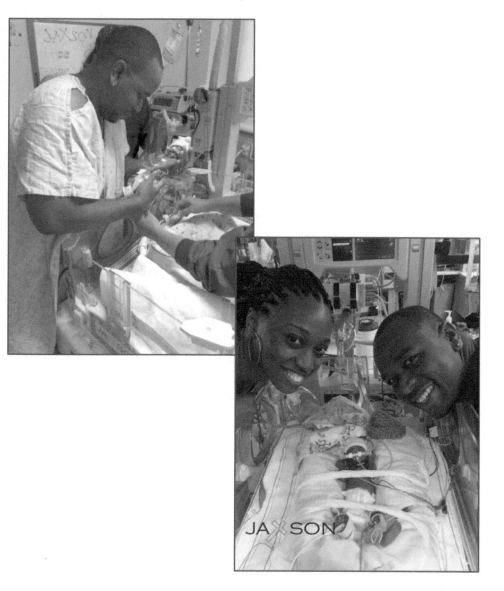

Home Sweet Home

One month prior to Jaxson coming home we had a celebration to celebrate Jaxson's birth. AKA my (very delayed) Baby shower! Obviously because of his extremely early birth, a traditional baby shower went out the window and I was bummed about it. I even went back and forth about having any type of celebration because I was grieving my pregnancy being cut short and having a tough time pivoting. I also felt a little guilt celebrating while Jaxson was still in the NICU having a tough time. That's truly where my focus was — on his health. I was scared that if we celebrated and got gifts that something bad would happen. Sounds irrational, I know, but these are the thoughts and feelings that go through a Preemie Mom's mind.

Ultimately, I threw myself into the planning process and worked through my fears. Jaxson had come so far and deserved to be celebrated. We also needed essentials for him. We had a baby registry and so many people wanted to bless our Family. So although I didn't have my huge baby bump, the celebration was beautiful. We had a slideshow with pictures of our journey in the NICU. We played games. We had the most delicious food and desserts, and got the chance to bask in the love of our Family and Friends.

Our village truly showed up and showed out for us. We received so many gifts and diapers, we literally didn't have to buy any for almost 7 months! It was amazing. I always encourage Preemie Moms to celebrate their baby, celebrate themselves, and celebrate the journey. It might not look like what you originally thought it would, or what you planned, (which sucks, I know). But your baby deserves to be celebrated, and so do you. Most people want to contribute to your child's life so I say let them. It takes a village to raise a child and if your village is there wanting to help, let them!

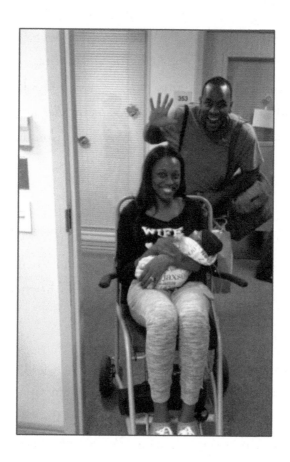

BRINGING JAXSON HOME

After 119 days, on November 14, 2015 *(which was the day before my original due date)*, Jaxson was discharged!!! HOME SWEET HOME!

This was the day we had prayed for and it had finally come. Our desire was for Jaxson to come home in time for the holidays. We also didn't want him to be in the NICU during Respiratory Syncytial Virus (RSV) season. RSV causes infections of the lungs and respiratory system, and it usually occurs during the Fall and Winter months. One of the Neonatologists used to look at us crazy when we would say, *"Our son will be home by his due date!"* Or *"Our son will be home for the Holidays!"* We were speaking it into existence.

As the days drew near we worked hard at bottle feeding and breastfeeding. One of the main requirements for him to come home was having the ability to suck, swallow and breathe. He had to take all of his feeds orally without a drop in his heart rate or oxygen saturations.

It took about 4 weeks for Jaxson to master this skill. We worked with the Speech Therapist and Occupational Therapist *(alongside his Nurses who were such a huge help)*. The end of the NICU journey can feel just as tough as the beginning. By the time Jaxson was ready to come home, he was the oldest baby in the NICU. It had been 4 months and all of the other babies that we started with had already gone home. So, he was moved to the 'growers and feeders' side of the NICU and the other babies were smaller, and required more attention just like Jaxson did in the beginning stages.

As a 4-month-old, he was awake more often, very alert, wanted to be held, didn't like the tubes and wires, etc. Also, his Nurse wasn't able to hold him all day, so that was tough on my Mama heart. Marc and I were still juggling work until it was time for him to come home. But we always made sure to help with his night time cares and loved on him really well before bedtime. We couldn't wait to bring our boy home!

Like many Preemies, Jaxson came home on oxygen, a pulse oximeter monitor (which monitors the baby's oxygen saturation levels), and 4 medications. A few days prior to his discharge, Life Care Solutions dropped all of the equipment off that we would need and taught my Husband how to use it. I was at work during the drop off and had to be briefed later.

I walked into my living room and immediately became overwhelmed seeing the multiple oxygen tanks and supplies. A warm sensation came upon me and I felt like I was going to pass out. I had hoped Jaxson's lungs would be strong enough to not require any more supplemental oxygen. This was just another part of our journey, and it was temporary. But when I initially saw the equipment it was a lot to digest.

I cried out to God, as I was feeling completely overwhelmed at what was ahead. I tried to wrap my head around Marc and I being responsible for Jaxson and needing special care. For 4 months, he was primarily being taken care of by Nurses, Doctors and Therapists who were experts. These people were trained for this and we weren't so it was very intimidating.

Yes, bringing him home is absolutely what we wanted, but we were still terrified and wanted to make sure we were properly prepared. I also pondered how we would be able to live a *"normal"* life. What would outings and play dates look like? Would I feel ashamed or embarrassed when we went out in public because we have oxygen and a pulse ox with us? There was so much that I had to process and mentally prepare for.

So, I put on my big girl panties again and got excited about learning everything necessary to bring him home. The entire journey showed me that God never gives us more than we can bear. He chose Marc and I to be Jaxson's Parents and had been equipping us all along. I felt the Lord's grace covering me and that's what helped me through. To know that God trusted us enough to not only birth a miracle, but to take care of him and raise him to be an amazing person showed me how blessed we were. It's truly all about perspective.

Many are called, but few are chosen. Knowing that you have been chosen and hand-picked by God to be your child's parent is amazing! No matter how hard the road you may have to travel, God's grace is sufficient. Read that again. His grace is simply enough. He doesn't call the equipped — He equips the called. The task that was upon us felt heavy. It was intense knowing that we would not only be parents providing a loving and nurturing environment, but also monitoring oxygen saturations, heart rate, multiple medications around the clock, and appointments. We were up for the challenge though.

The fact that Jaxson was healthy enough to come home with JUST a nasal cannula and medications was a MIRACLE! So much could have been worse. My husband and I don't have medical backgrounds, but for 4 months while Jaxson was in the NICU, God filled us with all of the knowledge we would need for this next phase of the journey. We would hold conversations with people and they would say, *"Wow, you sound like a Nurse!"* While we aren't certified RN's, we became skilled at taking care of Jaxson and gained the confidence and strength to be the best parents to our NICU graduate.

The week that he was set to be discharged we learned how to administer his medication. We learned how to switch out his nasal cannulas and pulse ox on his little toes. We learned how to operate his oxygen and heart rate machines. We took a CPR class at the Hospital which was required for all parents taking their baby home from the NICU. We even got our house deep cleaned. We also created a schedule using his NICU schedule as a blueprint. We basically adjusted it to fit our lifestyle. But feedings and medication were every 3 hours as well as diaper changes unless he had a blow out!

Because I worked for two of the four months while Jaxson was in the NICU, I was able to take maternity leave/baby bonding time. I was beyond grateful to have that opportunity because it was truly needed. Most women take the first 6 weeks off work with paid time to bond after delivery. This honestly is not enough time, in my opinion. But that's what most jobs allow here in the United States. I was off for 8 weeks following Jaxson's birth due to having a c-section. I used disability time and then went right back to work. It was tough juggling the roles of a Career Woman and a NICU Mom. I would wake up early, pump breastmilk, go to the NICU to be there for morning rounds, and then rush off to work by 9/10am.

On the days I had an early work day, Marc would go to the morning rounds and then fill me in. I would work all day, pumping milk in between meetings and what not, calling the NICU to check on Jaxson and then leave work and go straight to the NICU to be there for Jaxson's evening touch times and cares. Most of the time Marc would meet me there or we would ride together. This was our routine for 2 months until Jaxson came home. Our days were so long, but again, it was a sacrifice I made so that I could take time off when he came home.

Bringing Jaxson home was an exciting time and something we worked hard on preparing for. Little did we know that, with all of the preparations we would still have a lot of adjusting to do. You see, most NICU babies have a hard time adjusting to being at home initially. Home is quiet, peaceful, and darker. The babies become accustomed to loud noises, the beeps from the machines and people talking and constantly checking on them every three hours. So when Jaxson came home it was a little hectic!

For starters, he was four months old actually, but adjusted by just one day since he came home the day before his original due date. 'Actual Age' is your baby's real age, calculated from their birthday. 'Adjusted Age' is calculated from their due date. A baby needs a full 40 weeks to grow and develop, so the adjusted age takes into account the weeks of pregnancy that are missed due to a premature delivery. So that means for Jaxson, he was developmentally a newborn when he came home.

It was challenging trying to get him settled at home. He cried a lot, didn't want to sleep in his bassinet and wanted to be held all the time. It was interesting because while he was in the NICU, he was only held every three hours at a time and the rest of that time he was in an open crib. Day time was fine, but nighttime is when the real party began! We had this really nice Halo bassinet and he hated it. He only wanted to sleep on Marc's chest with the hall light on.

I didn't get great sleep at night because I had to pump, and keep an eye on Jaxson's monitor, plus prepare his bottles and medicine for the following day. Most nights we felt like we were running around in circles just trying to do everything we could to help Jaxson get comfortable. Marc was still working and he would get about 4 hours of sleep before having to head to work. I would nap with Jaxson in the mornings since that's when he slept best. We were really exhausted! But so overjoyed to have our miracle boy home.

Eventually we got into a routine but that first month at home, we definitely experienced true newborn hazing. On top of making sure his numbers (heart rate and oxygen saturations) remained balanced. We also had to make sure his bottles were prepared properly with the exact number of calories he was supposed to intake along with his medications. It was intense and I still look back and marvel at how well Marc and I worked as a team to make sure Jaxson was well taken care of and loved.

What helped Jaxson get acclimated to our home was having night lights all throughout our little townhouse. And there was a toy we had introduced him to while in the NICU that became a lifesaver once he was home. It was the Baby Einstein Sea Dreams soother. Jaxson loved that little thing so much. The little sea creatures would float around and there were 5 different settings for soothing sounds and music. He was also able to sleep laying down in his pack and play which we had to make extra comfy for him.

Not long after we were home, our days were also filled with lots of Pediatric appointments. We had to get his blood drawn every couple of weeks to make sure that his body was responding well to the medication he was on. As he grew that would mean his dosage would change, so checking his blood let us know what adjustments needed to be made, if any. Also, because he was such a tiny Preemie and born at such an early gestation, his pediatrician wanted to see him weekly to make sure that he was doing well.

In addition to this, for 8 weeks following discharge he had to get his eyes checked by his Ophthalmologist to make sure his eyes were developing well following his ROP surgery. We also had to get him set up with the Regional Center to start Early Intervention services. Because of Jaxson's birth weight and early gestation he qualified for certain therapies to help with his developmental milestones.

So, as you can see, my baby bonding time was filled with so much responsibility and oftentimes I felt like it was hard to just focus on bonding. These are the realities of bringing a premature baby home. Like I said, it's a blessing but also has so many moving parts. It truly required us to be organized, coordinated and on top of things.

PART III

Life In The NICU

SURVIVAL GUIDE

The Truth Behind Being
A Miracle Mama

Honestly speaking, prior to our journey I never fully knew that joy and sorrow could coexist. Joy for birthing this miracle, and sorrow for things not turning out the way you planned. I was mourning my pregnancy that was cut short, yet still so in love with seeing my baby boy grow outside of me.

You see, there's a deep void that comes with being a parent to a Preemie and you have to learn to cope even if you don't feel like it. Birthing a premature child puts you in a club that you didn't really want to be in, but you learn to embrace it. I remember in the beginning I had shut down in a way. I showed strength but inside I was a little withdrawn.

I couldn't talk to my friends who were pregnant. It was hard to see mothers with their babies out and about. My text replies were short and sweet, and talking on the phone was a rare occurrence. I became guarded not wanting people to feel pity for me, my husband or our baby boy. So you take all of these emotions and add in hormones and whew, you start to feel a little crazy!

I hid my truth for some time. To say I was as fragile as a piece of china would be putting it lightly. I felt like screaming at the top of my lungs sometimes. I wanted people to stop complaining about little things and realize that their life wasn't all that bad. I guess in a way I had some self-pity. I struggled with guilt and feeling like my body had failed.

People often mentioned how strong my husband and I were and their words would soothe my soul. I found strength from God when I looked at our son. He was a little fighter and that alone gave me the push I needed every single day. Our *"normal"* wasn't normal to most — but being honest and sharing our story as things were still unfolding helped people connect to us and in turn they blessed us as well. God didn't want me to be a regular Mom — he wanted me to be a Miracle Mama. He has used and is still using my story as someone else's survival guide. So, if what we went through is used for HIS glory, then I'm alright with that.

It took time (almost 2 years to be exact), to get pass those feelings of failure. And I know there are so many other Miracle Mama's who experience those same emotions. Especially when your baby is born prematurely although you know you did everything right. You can feel as though your body failed to keep your baby growing. While what you are feeling is valid, feelings aren't facts!

Our bodies did not fail us. We are not failures. We carried AND brought forth life. What a miracle! The love that I shared with my Husband created an amazing little boy. That, my friends, IS success. Not only that, I was able to provide nutrients for him with my breastmilk for 6 months of his life which was also a miracle. Many Preemie moms struggle with milk production, so I grew to appreciate my body.

While our plans changed drastically and caused us to readjust completely, I wouldn't change any of it. We had to endure so many hard things and Jaxson had a rough start. But God knew when he formed Jaxson in my womb that He would use his life to show the world that miracles still happen. Through our journey we provided hope to others. If you know anything about the Lord, you know He doesn't fail. His plans are perfect and I am grateful for what He has done for us.

Please don't let guilt get the best of you. Don't let someone else's journey make you feel inferior. So many times we as people get caught up focusing on someone else's life and it can make us feel like maybe we aren't doing enough or like you're failing. Remember, comparison is the thief of joy! I want you to know that you are amazing, and each day we are given the grace to handle whatever may come our way.

While your birth plan may have drastically been altered, please, do not beat yourself up. I know it's hard to watch your child lay in a hospital bed with tubes and wires, while you feel helpless. I know you may feel like you could have done something differently for your baby but that's not always the case so again — please, don't beat yourself up. Think about how awesome your baby is and what a miracle they are. The NICU journey is a marathon, not a sprint. So, take things one day at a time Mama, you got this!

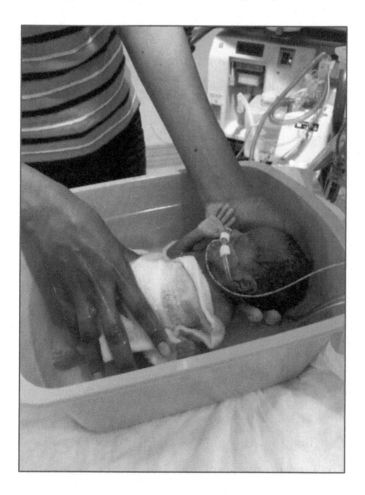

Being Your Baby's Advocate

Prior to becoming a Mom, I never considered myself as an Advocate. Did I have strong feelings about some things? Certainly! I stood up for good causes and I have never been afraid to speak up. But when you become a Mom and are responsible for someone else's wellbeing, it hits different! Once I started going into preterm labor it was almost as if something immediately switched and clicked in my brain that lit this fire in me.

I wasn't afraid to speak up regardless of whether I knew the lingo or not. I really just relied on God to speak through me to be able to advocate for me and my unborn son at the time. When I told my former OB to save my son, I knew then that I was being called to do hard things. Things that were scary and that had uncertain outcomes. All I knew is that I had a responsibility to do them.

There were times in the NICU when we would have meetings with the Doctors and they would try to tell us negative things about Jaxson. That was very hard to deal with, because we were battling their words against our faith. It's not that I didn't want to hear what they had to say; I more so wanted them to know that we were believing for a positive outcome and we were maintaining a positive mindset. I've talked to other NICU/Preemie Parents and they say how intimidated they feel because they don't have the medical knowledge. Or they feel like they don't have the right to question a Doctor or Nurse. To that I always say,

"This is your baby. You are their Parent. Yes, the Doctor has knowledge and went to school, but as a Parent you have instincts. You have power and you can't be so intimidated that you don't walk in that power and really allow yourself to be who your child needs you to be."

There was no time for me to sit back and cower down, or be so nervous to challenge some of the things that were said. As a Mother, it's my job to be Jaxson's voice. My job has always been to make sure he is getting everything that he needs and deserves. Some call it being a 'Mama Bear,' and that's cool. However, I just feel like our children need us to be their voice when they don't have one.

At the very least if you don't know something, you have a right to ask. You have a right to get a second opinion. You have a right to want to take a moment to think about what the medical professionals are saying or suggesting. You can be a strong advocate without being disrespectful or condescending. Another part of being your baby's advocate means asking other Preemie parents questions and researching things on your own.

Guarding yourself with knowledge is vital so that you know some of the terms that may be mentioned and won't feel completely lost. I feel like there's a fine line when it comes to advocating. I don't think it means operating out of defiance towards your doctors. However, I believe your role is to partner with them to do what's best for *your* Child.

The goal when on the NICU journey is to get the baby healthy and strong enough to go home! If everyone is on the same page then things will be ok. But again, I do know how it is to walk in those doors and sometimes feel like the team of expert professionals might be against you, or that you just aren't gelling well. If that's ever the case, speak with the Charge Nurse.

I think it's important to pick your battles and not fight over everything, but if you ever have serious concerns, ask for a meeting. This can be arranged with the NICU Social Worker/Hospital Advocate. Their job is to help you navigate this journey. Though they may not work directly with your baby, they are just as much a part of your Team as the others. You don't have to go through any of this alone, so use the resources that are available to you.

I firmly believe that a parent's instincts are real. Now sometimes we do have to weed out some of our personal feelings to make sure that our own traumas and fears are not overriding the situation. That's where that fine line of what is best and what will benefit your child comes into play. And I get totally it. I get the frustration because I've been there myself. But like I said, I think that you have to work really hard to put yourself in a mindset where you focus on the common goal which is to take your baby home. You cannot let your personal feelings get in the way of rationale.

I was also able to become a better advocate because I was empowered by other women who have come before me and went through the NICU journey. It encouraged me to speak up, to stay strong and express my expectations and concerns. Being connected to other Preemie Parents and dialoguing with someone who has been or is in your shoes can be very comforting and empowering. Although going through the NICU seems like it will never end, it does. It's a huge part of your journey, but it's not the only part in the grand scheme of things.

As Jaxson has gotten older, I have become skilled at advocating for him. There were times when I struggled to find my footing in the beginning of our NICU journey. But once I placed my feet completely on the ground, I became unstoppable. Though he has gotten older, I still go hard for my son. Jaxson will have what he needs. He will have the very best. He will have what he wants, and what's best for him.

Advocating is not easy — it's one of the hardest things about being a Preemie Mom, but I know that it is so worth it. What I do for him is setting him up for success. I am speaking on his behalf and being led ultimately by the Holy Spirit. And that's what gives me confidence to advocate for him boldly.

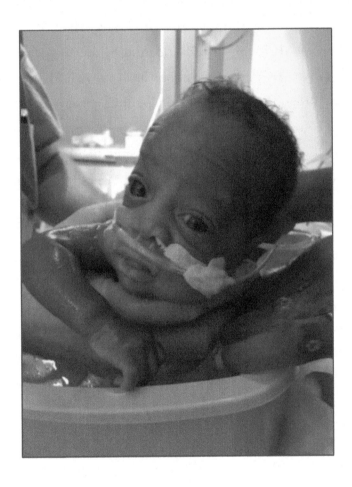

NICU 101

I knew little to nothing about the NICU which is why I want to take a moment to give you some helpful information. I believe you will find value in this for you or someone you may be supporting through the NICU rollercoaster experience. Our experience is about us having a micro Preemie in the NICU, but note that this information can also be useful for babies with other medical challenges outside of being born prematurely. I feel a big responsibility to share what I have learned. We didn't get any type of heads up or crash course UNTIL we were hit head on with the untimely circumstance.

The first 3 weeks were the toughest I would say as I was dealing with healing from my emergency c-section and adjusting to this new life. Watching my tiny 1lb 2.9oz baby fighting for his life day in and day out was extremely difficult. Through this, I learned that I was capable of enduring and overcoming hardship. We were introduced to medical terms, beeps, alarms and questions. There were many back and forth trips to the NICU, surgery, a transport to a children's hospital, sleepless nights and MORE! Looking back, I'm amazed at how we made it through. I am even more grateful that I can now pour into the lives of others.

TIPS FOR NAVIGATING THE NICU

1. **Ask questions...lots of them! No question is too big or small. Remember, you are new to this and by the time your little one breaks out of the NICU you will be a pro!**

Common Questions:
- What's the plan of care for my baby?
- How is their sugar level?
- How is their blood pressure?
- Are there any major concerns that we should know about?
- What would require a blood transfusion?
- Is my baby on caffeine? If so, why? How long do you expect them to be on it?
- How is their lung function?
- Is my baby tolerating their feedings? What's the feeding protocol/schedule?

2. **Here are a few common issues that occur in Preemies.**

There is PDA, Brady's, Apnea, ROP (Retinopathy of Prematurity), Hernias (Inguinal & umbilical), brain bleeds (Grades 1-4), pulmonary hypertension, CLD (chronic lung disease), slow weight gain, NEC, trouble feeding orally (by breast or bottle) and jaundice.

3. If your baby is receiving oxygen a daily a question to ask is: what's my babies saturation level?

There are different types of oxygen support that a baby requires depending on how developed their lungs are. They may be intubated — which means a tube is inserted down their throat and connected to a ventilator (conventional or oscillator). The oxygen support can be adjusted to provide breathing support to 100%. If your baby is intubated and their lung functioning improves, they will then be extubated — which means the breathing tube will be taken out of their throat and they will then be placed on a form of CPAP or high flow oxygen.

If your baby is on any form of these machines that is awesome! It means that they are doing some breathing on their own but need some assistance. Try not to get discouraged if it takes your baby a while to get extubated and put on any other form of oxygen, or even allowed to be on room air.

Lung function in Preemies takes time and while some babies excel faster it doesn't mean that your little one won't. There are medications that can aid in your Preemie's lung advancement. Some common interventions are: Lasix, Diuril, Steroids (DART protocol, dexamethasone, hydrocortisone). It's best to discuss with the NICU team what options would be best for your baby.

4. The NICU can be a noisy place.

We had 2 very different experiences as Jaxson spent 3 weeks at a level 3 NICU at a Children's hospital before being transferred back to his birth hospital. At one hospital there was a big room with about 8-10 babies. There was rarely a quiet moment as you can imagine a room filled with babies, monitors, families, nurses, doctors and respiratory therapists (RT). That room was definitely an intense place to be in. Things were completely different at Jaxson's birth hospital. Each baby had a private room with 1 nurse attending to 1 or 2 babies and the RT would sit outside the door at their workstation.

We definitely appreciated this type of atmosphere as it gave our son a chance to be in his own space without too much noise. We created a peaceful atmosphere in his room by speaking in low tones, playing worship and classical music, praying and keeping any negativity OUTSIDE OF THE ROOM.

I was able to bring in a comfortable recliner to put by his bedside, and do kangaroo care privately. Because premature babies are still developing, too much stimulation and activity surrounding their space can cause them to become overwhelmed. Their nervous system is still developing therefore dim lighting and low noise levels are vital.

I am also a firm believer that being in a positive atmosphere is vital to not only your health but that of your baby as well. Any time the Doctor had something BIG to tell us or something unfavorable, I asked that we speak outside of Jaxson's room. Negativity would not be spoken over my son, and my husband and I were very adamant about that! So, with that said, I encourage you to create a peaceful atmosphere even if you are in a room full of other babies without strict privacy. And try not to dwell on the negative things. Remember, your baby is fighting for their life and doing the best they can.

5. Get to know the NICU staff!

It helps a great deal to speak and be kind to all personnel staff you encounter in the NICU. After all, these people are all in direct connection with getting your baby on the road to good health and being able to go home and thrive. Find out who the Charge Nurse is, as well as the Neonatologist/Residents, Respiratory Therapist, Receptionist, Nurses, Social Worker and Physical/Occupational Therapist.

You are a part of your baby's medical team. You are their parent and their advocate. Your role isn't necessarily to become *friends* with the medical staff, but being cordial and letting them know your expectations is perfectly OK! Also, don't hesitate to ask for a *parent meeting* to discuss the plan of care, or share any concerns you may have. You are your baby's biggest advocate, so use your voice :).

6. If you are unsure of Anything, ASK!

I can't stress this one enough! If you have a concern that needs to be addressed due to the way your baby is being taken care of, SPEAK UP! Talk to the Charge Nurse. If they don't do anything, ask to speak with the Nurse Manager or Supervisor. Also, be sure to inform your baby's social worker or case manager. It is so, so, so important that everyone stays on the same page and works together as a team. The ultimate goal is to be able to bring your baby home once they are healthy enough. Don't be afraid to ask questions and seek clarification if you don't understand something.

Now, I'm not suggesting that you behave in a rebellious manner, or challenge every word the Doctor or Nurse says. More so, I want you to know that there is nothing wrong or inappropriate with knowing the details of your child's medical condition, and getting clarity on how to support them during this journey. Trust me, having a premature child is scary enough but what would be even scarier is if you are unaware about what is going on daily with your baby.

7. Ignorance is not bliss in the NICU!

While I know some things we may not want to know or even ask the Doctor out of fear of their answer, you will have to find a way to tackle that fear anyway.

8. Be open to receiving support from your spouse or partner during this time.

Even the strongest relationships may be tested due to lack of sleep, the stress of the situation, busy schedules and coping with a new routine. Emotions run high when your child is in the hospital. It is mentally exhausting when you are unsure of what the next minute or even next day holds.

Some couples get closer during this time and others drift apart. One parent may be more emotionally connected while the other struggles with visiting or being fully involved in the care of the baby. Extend grace to one another. Talk about how you are feeling. Go on a date. Do whatever it takes to stay connected during this time.

9. Make every moment count.

Life is so precious and having a child admitted in the NICU or PICU certainly puts things into perspective. During this time you will discover who and what really matters. You won't sweat the small things because you will understand just how quickly things can change. Try to stay in the moment.

When you visit your child, really allow yourself to be present. I shut out the world whenever I was in Jaxson's room. There was no talking on the phone or texting unless I was sending a message to my husband to give an update. We took photos and videos to capture special moments to share at a later time. But while we were in his room, we tried our very best to focus on him — The world could wait.

Here are some opportunities for you to connect with your baby during your visit:

- bath time
- taking their temperature
- changing their diaper
- feeding

These moments will help you really feel like an active participant and parent. It's not unusual for parents to feel like they aren't *real* parents during their time in the NICU, because their child is being cared for by others. But remember, YOU *are* their parent. Try not to shut down. While your baby does need the care of the Nurses and Doctors, they still need YOUR love! Love heals.

More Ways To Connect With Your Baby:

- Kangaroo care: This is very important for the health and development of your child. It also helps create a bond like none other. Do this every chance you get!

- Read to your baby. This aids with brain development also and creates a sense of normalcy.
- Pray over them, daily! I wasn't ashamed to rest my hands on Jaxson's incubator and pour out my heart to God. I would even lay hands on my son through the two small openings. I asked God to protect, bless and continue to breathe life into my son. PRAYER WORKS!
- Play music in your baby's space. Inspirational, classical, gospel, jazz and lullabies are popular and good options. This helps soothe them and can also aid in brain development.
- Talk to your little miracle! While they may not be able to respond they are listening!

10. Take care of yourself.

You are not a bad parent if you choose to take a few hours out of your day to do something nice for yourself. Go get a manicure and/or pedicure. Take a nap at home. Go enjoy a dessert or cup of coffee. Go see a movie. Have a date with your spouse. Just do something for YOU!

At 7 days post-partum, before going to visit Jaxson for the day, we went to the beach for a couple of hours. I desperately needed the vitamin D and a moment to just breathe in the fresh air. Doing this BEFORE going to the hospital put me in a good mood and head space to face the NICU and what the day would bring.

Even if you don't feel up to doing any of the things suggested above, just please take care of yourself. Recovering from the birth process and going through the NICU requires extra care for your body and your mind. If you don't take care of yourself, you may end up sick or having a harder recovery period. Please don't let guilt consume you. If you need to a break, take one!

The NICU is where I found my strength — where I learned what true love and sacrifice meant. It was the place where Jesus literally held my hand day in and day out, as we watched Him perform a miracle for our baby boy. NICU is also a place where the nights are long and often lonely. But it can be a place where you experience tiny miracles along the way. It is a place where joy and sorrow can coexist — a place where you hold onto hope for dear life.

Those hard yet inevitable days are all a part of the process. Once you make it out, you will have an immense amount of gratitude for the journey. I learned to not take anything for granted and to celebrate everything whether big or small. As your Preemie grows and you see them smiling, laughing and thriving, you will think of the days that you all have overcome.

We are currently living in answered prayers and 6 years later I am still so grateful. Grateful for every miracle I have seen during our 119 day NICU stay and beyond.

PREPARING TO BRING YOUR
BABY HOME FROM THE NICU

- DEEP CLEAN YOUR HOUSE: Hire someone to come and take this load off of you if you don't want to do it yourself. I'm an advocate for deep cleaning because you want your house to be as fresh and sterile as possible.

- NIGHT LIGHTS: You definitely want to have several on hand to put in the room the baby will be sleeping in. Remember, they are used to a well lit environment, so complete darkness may bother them and affect their sleep.

- SOUND MACHINE: White noise such as soothing sounds of the ocean waves, lullaby, etc. is perfect to help your little one fall asleep and have a good rest.

- BE FLEXIBLE & PATIENT: Don't stress about everything being perfect! I know that can be easier said than done. But really, try to enjoy the moment. If you go into this already knowing that the first few weeks may be challenging, I think that helps you not be caught off guard (like we were). The nursery may not be perfect or even finished for that matter. But, honestly, they may not even sleep in there when you first come home! What your baby needs is a clean and safe environment. All the other *"stuff"* can wait.

• GIVE YOURSELF GRACE: This is new for your baby and your Family. It will take time to get into a groove. Don't beat yourself up if you don't know everything. Take things one day at a time. You may not be able to complete your to-do list in one day and that too is OK. Take a walk with your baby and get some fresh air. Try to carve out time for self-care. Taking good care of yourself and filling your cup will help you be the best Mom you can be.

• FIND A PEDIATRICIAN: Prior to Jaxson's discharge, we had to have a Pediatrician and appointment scheduled for 2 days after leaving the NICU. This appointment is similar to the one full term newborns go to once they go home. They want to make sure the baby is eating well, gaining weight and overall adjusting well to life at home. I would definitely recommend searching for a Pediatrician that has experience with Preemies. I found Jaxson's Ped by asking a couple of Parents in the NICU and cross referencing with the NICU Team.

....A BIT OF ENCOURAGEMENT

If you find yourself wondering if the roller coaster will ever end, it will! There is light at the end of the tunnel. Brighter days await you outside of the NICU doors. It takes courage to remain positive and hope for the best. But, you have it in you. We all do. Sometimes it takes life changing situations to propel you into tapping into that unknown strength that's deep down within you.

I am stronger today than I was when I had Jaxson. My hope and faith grew to heights I never knew existed. And what's amazing is that I still carry it with me today. I can look back at our journey when I'm feeling down or discouraged and it serves as a reminder of God's faithfulness. That hope I gained still carries me and it's how I give it to others so freely. Because if God did it for me, He surely can do it for you!

Thank You

I want to Thank my Family for their love and support. To my Husband Marc: Thank you for always having my back and believing in me. The journey that we have taken on thus far has had God's hand all over it. I'm grateful that I get to do life with you and raise our beautiful Children. Thank you for giving me space to be who God created me to be, while also being your Wife.

To my Babies, Jaxson and Kamryn: Mommy loves you sooooo very much. I am thankful that God has entrusted me with you. You make me a better Woman and I pray you will always dream big and know that nothing is too hard with hope, faith, love and hard work!

To my Dad & Mom *(my Praying Mom to be exact)*: Thank you, Mom from the bottom of my heart for always being my number 1 fan and believing in me. You have spoken life and the goodness of God into me from the time I was born. I know without a shadow of a doubt that is it because of your prayers that God has shined His face on me. I'm grateful. Dad, thank you for instilling so many valuable principles in me, and pushing me to do great things in life. Your wealth of wisdom is appreciated.

Thank you to the NICU Staff at Little Company of Mary that saved my son's life, and helped us get the miracle we prayed for.

We are also very grateful for the NICU staff at Miller Children's Hospital.

Thank you to every person who has ever prayed for our Family, cheered for us, cried with us and supported us. We appreciate you and love you!

And to YOU, my Reader, thank you for reading the words of my heart and being open to receiving my experience. It is my hope and prayer that through the pages of the book, you will find strength and hope that you can carry into your daily lives.

Xo,

Need more proof that miracles happen?

Follow us on Instagram @jaxsonsmiracle | @imacarnelus

Shop Inspirational Apparel for Kids & Adults

halosandmiracles.com | @halosandmiracles

Made in the USA
Coppell, TX
09 December 2021